GREAT YA and GORLESTON

Beside the Sea

Colin Tooke

First Published 2001
by
Tookes Books
14 Hurrell Road
Caister-on-Sea
Great Yarmouth NR30 5XG
e-mail colin.tooke@rjt.co.uk

Other titles in this series:
The Past Fifty Years
Front Line Towns
Caister 2000 Years a Village
The Rows and Old Town

ISBN 0 9532953 4 6

Printed in England by Blackwell John Buckle
Charles Street, Great Yarmouth, Norfolk

Contents

Front Cover - *A Stroll along the Prom. July 1928*
Back Cover - *The Marine Parade c1910*

**My New Bathing Costume is rather attractive:
But I can't find a single man.**

One of the first things the holidaymaker did after arrival was to
relay the news to those back home of a safe journey. This was done
by a picture postcard, many of which showed views of the resort.
Another popular subject was the humorous card such as this example
which was sent from Great Yarmouth in 1919.

Introduction

Since the middle of the eighteenth century Great Yarmouth has attracted visitors as a seaside town. The early visitors came not for entertainment and holidays but for the benefit of their health at a time when 'taking the waters' was considered a remedy for a wide range of complaints and illnesses. Almost a hundred years were to pass before these visitors to the seaside began to enjoy themselves and find pleasure in their visits. Bathing was popularised by members of the Royal family and with the spread of the railway network, which has been said to have both popularised and vulgarised seaside resorts, many coastal towns developed a new industry. It required the Bank Holiday Act of 1871 to give the working classes the chance to get away from the drudgery of the Victorian industrial areas and for the first time experience the fresh air and freedom the seaside had to offer.

As more people came to the seaside so more amenities were built and entertainment flourished, from the original Nigger Minstrel shows on the beach to the 'big name' theatre shows of the 1950's and 60's. Hotels, apartments and boarding houses all opened their doors to the new generations of holidaymakers and a whole new industry flourished in a part of Great Yarmouth which, until the mid eighteenth century, had been a desolate expanse of sand and marram grass used only by fishermen and beachmen.

The holiday industry grew up over a period of two hundred and fifty years to reach a peak in the 1950's. Cheap foreign holidays and the mobility which increasing car ownership brought saw the beginning of a decline in the popularity of the traditional seaside holiday.

The Great Yarmouth Seafront Regeneration Project began work in 1999 to seek ways to transform the seafront and maintain the town's position as the third largest seaside resort in the UK and one of the countries leading holiday destinations. Pedestrianised paved areas, a wider Esplanade and the introduction of a light tramway system are but a few of the proposals designed to attract more people. The traditional seaside 'bucket and spade' holiday has been in a steady decline for many years and the English Tourism Council is encouraging resorts to broaden their outlook to lure more visitors. The following pages look back to the origins of Great Yarmouth as a seaside resort and follow its fortunes through to its heyday in the 1960's.

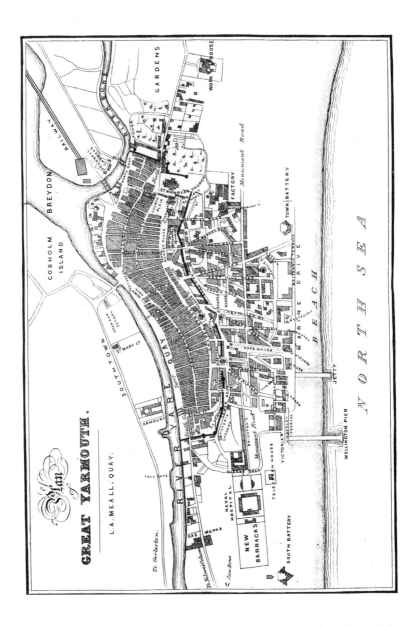

This map was published in a *Guide to Great Yarmouth* in 1858 and was drawn before the Britannia Pier had been built and only a few years after the Marine Parade had been constructed. It shows the limited amount of development outside the town walls at that time, a time when the town was beginning to emerge as a holiday resort.

Taking the Waters

In the mid eighteenth century Great Yarmouth was a small but densely populated town on the bank of the river Yare, its size having been restricted for over four hundred years by a medieval town wall. All the land between the town and the sea shore and the land at the southern end of the sand spit on which the town had been built was wind blown sand and marram grass, a bleak open area uninhabited for generations and known as the Denes. Tracks from the gates in the old town wall led across the Denes to a few windmills where the town's flour was ground and communal fresh water wells where many of the townsfolk went for their drinking water. Apart from this the town turned its back on the sea, the river being the important life line of a town already famous as the leading herring port in Europe. The Denes were traditionally used by the town's fishermen to lay out and dry their nets and by the ropemakers who required large open spaces to carry out their work. The sea was considered only as a source of food, a means of transport and in times of trouble a defence against foreign invaders. A small fishing community lived in cottages, known as cotes, on the beach near the high water mark, mainly clustered around the Jetty which had been built in 1560. In general the townsfolk remained within the old town keeping their houses as far away from the sea as possible.

In 1660 Doctor Robert White published information on the medicinal benefits of sea water, proclaiming it to be far better for ones health than the waters of the inland spa towns which had been patronised for many years by the rich and fashionable members of society. Spring water from the cliffs at Scarborough was said to cure asthma, open the lungs and purify the blood while sea water could cure gout and kill all manner of worms (a common complaint at that time). The idea of immersing the body in water of any kind was, at this time, predominantly for medicinal purposes, hence the spas were mainly patronised by invalids and the sick. Cleanliness among the general population left much to be desired and baths were only taken as a necessity, any ideas of bathing for pleasure were considered immoral.

Coastal towns slowly started to rival the inland spa towns as places to relax and attempt to find a cure for an untold number of ailments. The health giving powers of sea water and the sea air led the English aristocracy to the seaside, often in winter as immersion in

A painting of Yarmouth beach in 1795. This collection of fishermen's sheds and lookouts would have been clustered around the Jetty. It is possible that the original Bath House is one of the buildings shown here.

ice-cold water was thought to cure everything. Towns like Great Yarmouth were, although they did not recognise it, on the verge of a completely new social trend, the seaside visitor.

The first evidence of anyone visiting the town for medicinal reasons comes from a letter dated 23 September 1734, written by a Miss Longe and in which she says:

> *"I have gone into the sea every morning since my arrival here, I think myself much better for it which makes the dullness of the place less disagreeable".*

These few words herald the birth of a new seaside industry, although Miss Longe appeared not to be too impressed with her surroundings and the town would obviously have to improve its facilities if more visitors were to follow this young lady.

In 1753 a Doctor Russell at Brighton practised a new cure by urging his patients to 'use sea water for diseases of the glands'. To 'purify the belly' his advice was to drink large quantities of sea water, mixed with milk or honey if desired, as this would 'purge the body'. The results of this advice can be left to the imagination but it was taken seriously by many people and the seaside now became the fashionable retreat for the upper classes and those who had the time and the means to travel to 'take the waters'.

In 1760 the Norwich Mercury reported 'On Monday 19 May will be opened at Gt Yarmouth two commodious Sea Baths, supplied every morning from the sea'. This new Bath House contained two large plunge baths, one for ladies, one for gentlemen, each surrounded by dressing rooms. (Today the building housing the Flamingo amusements stands on the site of the original Bath House.) The baths soon gained popularity, visitors staying in the old town, patrons for the baths conveyed to the Bath House by a Yarmouth Coach, a gaily painted and modified version of the Yarmouth troll cart. Ladies could travel in the Bath House Fly, a four wheel carriage which could carry two passengers but was drawn by two men instead of horses. The Bath House was surrounded by the houses, storesheds and lookout towers of the fishermen and beachmen.

A winter scene on Yarmouth beach in 1821. The bathing machines have been pulled up above the high water mark. By this time more substantial and larger buildings have appeared along what would later become the Marine Parade.

THEATRE, YARMOUTH.

By His Majesty's Servants from the Theatre-Royal, Norwich.

On *SATURDAY*, *7th June*, 1803.

Will be presented A DRAMA, called, The

Castle Spectre

(With new & appropriate Scenery, Dresses, and Decorations.)

Osmond,   Mr. BOWLES,
Reginald,   Mr. BEACHEM—Percy,   Mr. FITZGERALD,
Father Philip,   Mr. THOMPSON—Motley,   Mr. BENNETT,
Kenric,   Mr. ERRINGTON—Saib,   Mr. MANN,
Hassan,   Mr. SMITH—Muley,   Mr. MILES,
Allan,   Mr. WILDE—Edric,   Mr. BIRRELL.

Angela,   Mrs. BOWLES,
Alice,   Mrs. GROVE—Evelina,   Mrs. ERRINGTON.

To which will be added A FARCE, called, The

WEATHERCOCK.

Old Fickle,   Mr. THOMPSON,
Tristram Fickle,   Mr. BENNETT—Briefwit,   Mr. BIRRELL,
Sneer,   Mr. BEACHEM—Gardener,   Mr. GREEN,
Barber,   Mr. MILES.

Variella, (with Songs)   Mrs. BINFIELD,
Ready,   Mrs. FITZGERALD.

To begin at SEVEN O'CLOCK.

Days of playing...Monday...Tuesday...Thursday...& Saturday.

Lower Boxes 4s.... half-price 2s.   ‖   Pit 2s. 6d.....half-price 1s. 6d.
Upper Boxes 3s.....half-price 1s. 6d.   Gallery 1s.....half-price 6d.

TICKETS to be had of MR BEART, Printer; and of MR. STANNARD, at the Theatre; of
whom places for the Boxes may be taken from Eleven 'till One.

BEART, PRINTER, QUAY, YARMOUTH.

The only entertainment in the early nineteenth century was at the Theatre Royal on Theatre Plain. This poster for June 1803 advertises the drama and farce on offer for that week.

As its popularity increased a large public room was added to the building and by 1788 daily newspapers were available for the patrons. Here they could also enjoy 'the salubrious sea breezes'. From the end of May until the middle of October the 'genteel company' would assemble in the evenings to listen to music, play billiards and on occasion partake of balls, tea-parties and public breakfasts, all probably to the great amusement of the local fishing community. The business of entertaining people at the seaside had begun.

Bathing machines appeared on the beach, giving an alternative method of immersing the body in seawater. The machine (basically a wooden hut on wheels) was pulled into the sea by a horse and the 'bather' emerged down some steps to immerse themselves in the sea, sometimes with the help of ladies known as 'dippers', while enjoying a certain amount of privacy given by the machine. This practice was given the Royal seal of approval in 1789 when George III used a bathing machine at Weymouth, where his doctors had advised the treatment to try and cure his bouts of madness, alas to no avail.

In 1778 the town's first theatre, the Theatre Royal, opened on Theatre Plain. This provided for the first time some good quality enter-tainment for both the residents of the town and the visitors. By the end of the eighteenth century many seaside towns had acquired bath houses and bathing machines and the seaside had become firmly established as the place to seek medicinal cures and to enjoy the fresh sea air. Still only people of the 'upper classes', those with the time and money, could partake in these pursuits, the ordinary working people would have to wait several years before they too could visit the seaside.

From the beginning of the nineteenth century the town began to expand outside the confines of the old town wall onto the Denes, and to accommodate the increasing number of visitors closer to the seashore, lodging houses began to appear. The town's first seaside lodging houses were at Ansells Buildings (later to become the site of the Empire cinema).

By 1835 the old baths at the Bath House had been removed and new ones installed, a number of small baths giving the choice of hot or cold sea water. The building was rebuilt and enlarged, part converted into a family hotel and lodging house, and was later to be known as the Bath Hotel. One of the earliest guides to the town was published in 1839 and in this the rate of subscription to the Bath House for the season was 15/- (75p) for gentlemen and 10/- (50p) for ladies.

The buildings along the sea front c1864. On the extreme left is Shadingfield Lodge and the white building in the centre of the picture is the Royal Hotel. To the right of this are four houses of which three were lodging houses. The detached house second from the right, with the flood wall in front, is the house of Mr George Palmer, South Beach Lodge, which was later demolished to allow the Gem (Windmill) to be built on the site. To the right of this the house with five windows on the first floor and the adjacent Steam Packet Tavern now form Harry Ramsden's Fish Restaurant.

Also available at the Bath House were vapour baths, medicated vapour baths and sulphurous or vinegar baths.

The strict conditions which had been imposed to restrict any development on the Denes were relaxed in 1810 and the Corporation leased land to the entrepreneurs who could foresee a rapid development in the emerging seaside industry. The Municipal Corporation Act of 1835 allowed more development on the Denes, new roads such as Regent Road were laid out and large residential buildings began to appear, the fishermen and beachmen were not now the only inhabitants of this once desolate area. Visits to the seaside become more popular and in 1841 the Times reported:

> *"There has been an increasing tendency of late years among all classes to find excuses for holidays. Among those who are well-to-do the annual trip to the seaside has become a necessity of which their fathers, or at least their grandfathers never dreamt."*

Charles Dickens recorded a scene at Ramsgate which could have applied to any seaside town in the mid nineteenth century:

"four young ladies, each furnished with a towel, tripped up the steps of a bathing machine. In went the horse, floundering about in the water; round turned the machine; down sat the driver; and presently out burst the young ladies aforesaid, with four distinct splashes."

In these pre-railway days to travel any distance was difficult, slow and not for the faint hearted. Coaches linked the town to London, Birmingham and the Midlands, Bury and Cambridge. The 'Star' coach to London left from the Quay at 7am every morning, travelling via Lowestoft and Yoxford to the Bull Inn at Aldgate and Regent Circus, Piccadilly. The Birmingham coach passed through Grantham, Leicester and Coventry, a journey of many hours. Another method of travel was by steam packet, these boats providing weekly services to and from London with the best cabin costing 13/- (65p) and a fore cabin 6/6d (35p). Another steam packet plied between Yarmouth and Hull each week.

In 1819 John Preston had written: "As a watering place there cannot be a more commodious one than Yarmouth, the beach is fine sand and the best constructed bathing machines are constantly in readiness. From the beginnings of June to the middle of October Yarmouth is much resorted to by families of gentility of Norfolk and Suffolk, as well as London and other parts of the kingdom and it abounds with convenient and elegant lodgings."By the beginning of Victoria's reign the seaside was slowly becoming a place for enjoyment rather than the unrelenting search for a medical cure.

PUBLIC BATHS.

BATH HOUSE

GREAT YARMOUTH.

The Public are respectfully informed that at the above premises, although holding by *Covenant* in their Lease under the Corporation of this Borough the

Sole Right for Sea Water Baths,

The Charges are below the average of other Sea Bathing places; viz., as under:—

Hot Sea Water Baths	..	2s. 0d.
Six do.	..	10s. 6d.
Twelve do.	..	£1 0s. 0d.
Shower do.	:	1s. 6d.
Six do.	..	7s. 0d

Daily in constant readiness : Sundays from 7 a.m. till 1 p.m.

A scene on Yarmouth beach in the 1860's with the Britannia Pier in the background. Note the formal clothes of top hat and crinoline dresses the Victorians are wearing on the beach. Sunbathing was not an option and every precaution was taken to prevent any bare skin being exposed to the sun. The bathing machines are fitted with 'modesty hoods' but would only have been used in the morning as bathing after 2pm was considered unsociable.

The Victorian Resort

The Victorian era heralded a revolution at the seaside with new ideas and new customs. In 1847 Queen Victoria wrote in her diary:

> *"Drove down to the beach with my maid and went into a bathing machine where I undressed and bathed in the sea for the first time in my life. A very nice woman attended me. I thought it delightful until I put my head under water when I thought I should be stifled."*

This was the first time a member of the royal family had bathed in the sea for pleasure and it was to make the practice acceptable to all, although for many years to come the sexes would be strictly segregated while bathing.

The first hotel to front the sea was the Royal Hotel, opened in 1841, the same year that a company known as the Victoria Building Company embarked upon an ambitious scheme at the south end of the town, a scheme which envisaged terraces of large elegant houses in a setting designed to attract people from the 'upper classes' to settle in the town. The Victoria Hotel (now the Carlton Hotel), the flagship building of the company, opened in 1842 and by 1849 Kimberly Terrace was completed This was followed by the development of Camperdown Place, a short street of small but tasteful houses, Albert Square and Brandon Terrace. In front of Kimberly Terrace an Esplanade and carriage way was laid. Unfortunately for the company the properties did not sell as expected, even the arrival of the railway (the line from Norwich into Vauxhall station) in 1844 did nothing to benefit the new development and long before its grand scheme could be completed the company was forced to stop building. The Wellington Arches, the gateway to the estate, stand today in Wellington Road. Although no further building was carried out the company was not finally wound up until 1968.

In 1848 another fine development, a terrace of private houses known as Britannia Terrace, was completed further north and nine years later a Marine Parade was constructed between this terrace and the Victoria Estate. New buildings soon appeared along the west side of the Marine Parade, in 1859 a Coastguard Station (now the site of the

Burton's *Looker-On and Visitors Register* 18 August 1860. This weekly paper was published and printed by William Dinzey Burton at 180 King Street and contained a list of visitors in the town that week, giving their names, where they came from and where they were staying. William Burton also ran a circulating library which he advertised as 'providing sea-side reading for fashionable visitors'.

Tower complex), a Lifeboat House to contain two lifeboats (now Ghostbusters) and a home for shipwrecked sailors (now the Maritime Museum). On land to the south of Kimberley Terrace a private residence, Sutherland Lodge (now Queen Elizabeth Court), was built in 1860 and the Assembly Rooms (now the Masonic Lodge) in 1863. These were closely followed by Shadingfield Lodge, a holiday home for a wealthy Suffolk family, the Cuddons. The Prince of Wales, later Edward VII and a friend of the family, stayed with them at Shadingfield Lodge several times towards the end of the century. Today this is a casino but it could also be described as the town's only Stately Home. A second railway came to the town in June 1859 when the East Suffolk Railway Company opened Southtown Station which within a few years was to offer a through service to London via Beccles in 2½ hours, a time which would be difficult to equal today.

The rapid expansion of the rail network meant increasing numbers of visitors and in 1868 the local Board of Health issued a set of by-laws which reflected the Victorian modesty of the period. No bathing was permitted after 2pm (this was the time of day Victorian ladies would 'promenade' along the Marine Parade), and all bathing machines, which by now were being used more for pleasure than medicinal purposes, had to be equipped with hoods so that bathers could not be seen from the beach. No person in a boat was allowed to moor or stop at sea within 300 yards of a bathing machine licensed for ladies, the penalty being £2. The Bath House with its indoor sea-water baths was still popular and in 1868 an engine house and reservoir were erected on the north side of the Jetty to provide a constant supply of fresh sea-water to the baths.

In a class-ridden Victorian society it was important for many to know who was staying in a resort and in common with other seaside towns at this period a list of visitors was published each week. A special newspaper, Burton's *Yarmouth Looker On and Visitors Register*, appeared in August 1860 and listed the names, home town, and guest house of the principal visitors.

In 1871 the Bank Holiday Act came into force giving the ordinary working man a chance to have a break from the drudgery of the factory, mill or mine and August Bank Holiday gave the opportunity for several thousand from London and the industrial Midlands to travel to the seaside. Excursion trains into Southtown and Vauxhall brought

Henry B Binko's Electric Railway ran from the Aquarium to the North Star Battery. The railway started on 27 July 1885 but was seized by the Bankruptcy Court on 10 August. This must be the shortest lived attraction ever in the town.

almost 83,000 people to the town that year. Victorian values still restricted behaviour to a certain extent but a Music Hall song of the day was correct when it said, "You can do all sorts of things at the seaside that you cannot do at home". In August 1877 the town's third railway station, known as Beach, was opened on land off Nelson Road (now the Coach Station) and this was soon to provide the town with a direct rail link to the north of England. The town was now served by three separate railway companies in addition to the several steam ships whose regular services brought many people from London to the town. This was also the year that work to widen the length of Marine Parade between the two piers by sixty feet was completed. At the junction of the Parade and Regent Road the impressive Queens Hotel (now the New Beach Hotel) was built in 1880.

In September 1876 an Aquarium was opened at the north end of the Marine Parade. From the position of the building and the fact that it faced south it is clear that the Corporation did not at that time expect the Parade to extend northwards. The building contained a large variety of

The original design for the Aquarium. The Winter Garden on the left would have stood where the front car park now is. A modified version of the remainder, with a flat roof and without the towers was opened on 5 September 1876 by Lord Suffield.

The Jetty in the late 1860's. The stalls are selling fish and the advertisements on the right are for Abraham Solomon, a jeweller and optician at 164 King Street and Blyth's the tobacconist in Broad Row.

fish in 18 tanks which varied in length from 17 feet to 50 feet. The smallest tank held 2,500 gallons of water, the largest 26,000 gallons. Ponds for crocodiles, alligators and seals were provided and over 300 tons of rocks were placed in and around the tanks and pools. The building also contained a reading room, private dining room and a reference room. On the flat roof was a roller skating rink which from time to time was turned into an ice rink. A small stage was added at one end to make an open air theatre. Lectures, concerts, military bands and light entertainment took place throughout the year and in 1881 HRH Prince of Wales attended a variety concert given by the London Gaiety Company on two successive days. The original plans had included a Winter Garden but lack of finance had restricted the scheme. By 1881 lack of public support for an aquarium and financial problems led to the company going bankrupt and the building was sold for £5,000.

In July 1883 a new Royal Aquarium opened. Considerable rebuilding had resulted in a new façade and it was now a theatre rather than an aquarium although some of the fish tanks had been retained. There was a Grand Hall, adaptable for circus performances, a Minor Hall (in 1934 to become the Little Theatre) and refreshment rooms complete with kitchens. As a theatre the building provided live entertainment, touring companies performing musical comedy, thrillers and variety throughout the year, this continuing until 1939. From 1954 a resident summer show was staged at the Royal Aquarium, the first being Ted Ray and Hilda Baker in a show which had to be moved there at the last minute following the loss of the Britannia Pier Pavilion by fire. Summer shows continued until 1967 when the theatre was closed for alterations, the stage was reduced in size and a new Cinemascope screen installed. The new cinema opened in May 1970 and at the same time the northern end of the building opened as the Dixieland Showbar (now Rosie's). The building has remained as a cinema, the name changing to the Royalty and from 1996 the Hollywood.

An 1883 guide book described the town thus:

"both as a port and watering place Yarmouth is by far the most important town on the coast of East Anglia. Hundreds of visitors annually make it their holiday quarters and in August thousands of excursionists are poured into it by rail and steamer."

The Beach Concert Party on the Central Beach in the 1880's before the high canvas screens were put around the 'ring'. At first Nigger Minstrels and later Concert Parties and Pierrot Groups provided this popular form of entertainment, a forerunner to the traditional Pier Pavilion Seaside Shows. Below, the Troubadours Concert Party perform in the 'ring' during the 1919 season.

Above a typical beach scene in 1892 and below a travelling menagerie on the beach the same year.

Boys with their goat carts waiting for customers near the Jetty in the late 1870's.
These carts were popular children's rides until they were banned in 1911. In the
background, from the right, is the Sailors Home, the Norfolk Hotel, the Telegraph
Office, a fish warehouse known as the Fish Station and part of the Bath Hotel. The
lookout belongs to the Young Company of Beachmen and was the tallest lookout along
the Marine Parade. The Norfolk Hotel is now The Shack while the Fish Warehouse and
the Telegraph Office form the Golden Nugget amusement arcade.

While the earlier Victorians had been happy enough to stroll along the promenade those arriving in the latter part of the century looked for more adventurous entertainment and a greater variety of amusements. In 1887 a Switchback Railway, a forerunner of the Scenic Railway, opened on a piece of land north of Euston Road. This proved very popular, a ride costing 3d for adults and 2d for children. As residential development spread northwards from the Royal Aquarium the Switchback had to keep moving further north until its last site, from 1900 until 1909 was between Beaconsfield Road and Salisbury Road. In 1890 another attraction, the Hotchkiss Bicycle Railway, opened on an adjacent site. This consisted of a circular track of two rails with six 'bicycles' on each, the rider propelling the machine by moving the pedals up and down, driving the front wheel. Both these rides remained until the 1909 season when they were moved to a site in Yorkshire.

Waste land between the Wellington Pier and the Jetty was laid out as gardens in 1891 with a promenade and seating adjacent to the beach. A bandstand was erected in the gardens and military bands played twice daily. The first amusement arcade on the seafront was opened in 1896 by the Barron family. The building, known as the Jubilee Exhibition, stood next to Goode's Hotel and contained side shows, slot machines and a rifle range, similar entertainment to that only previously seen at travelling fairs. This was also the first place in the town to show moving pictures, again entertainment only previously seen at fairgrounds. The following year Mr Warwick opened his Revolving Tower to the north of the Britannia Pier. A revolving cage capable of carrying 150 passengers travelled to the top of the 140 feet high tower where an observation platform provided panoramic views of the town and surrounding countryside. At the base of the Tower were Refreshment Rooms and Lavatories. On its reopening after the First World War the cage did not revolve and it became known as the Observation Tower but continued to be a popular attraction until demolished in 1941.

The Central Beach in 1891

In the last decade of the century there was a considerable investment in the development of pleasure, entertainment and public amenities in the town both by the Corporation and private investors. One man who was to play an important part in the development of the resort at this time was Mr John William Nightingale who came to the town in 1882 to take over as lessee of the newly refurbished Royal Aquarium. Within a few years Nightingale had built up an empire of business interests which included the Victoria, Royal and Queens Hotels, the Theatre Royal, Shadingfield Lodge and controlling interests in the Revolving Tower and the rebuilt Britannia Pier. One of his greatest successes was achieved as a caterer for large groups at the Royal Aquarium where up to 1000 people could be accommodated at one time. J W Nightingale died in 1911 after being deeply affected by the destruction of the fine Britannia Pier Pavilion two years earlier but his energy, foresight and enterprise had made him probably the most important and influential figure in the early days of Yarmouth's development as a seaside resort. He was succeeded by his son Walter and the family retained business interests in the town (the Queens Hotel) until the 1950's.

In 1899 a Sinuous Railway and Toboggan Slide were constructed on a site opposite the Royal Naval Hospital and as the town moved into the twentieth century it was clear that more adventurous amusements were on their way.

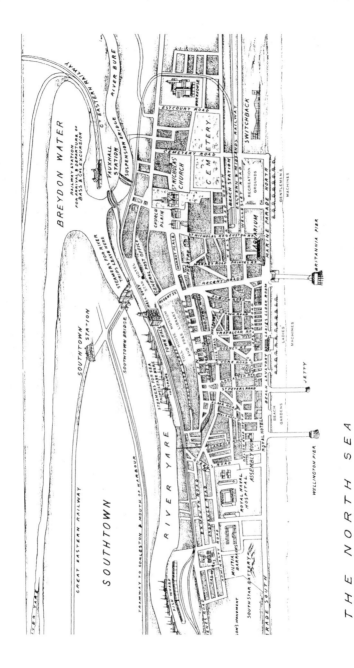

The street plan from a Yarmouth Guide of 1896.

An 1899 Holiday Diary

At the end of the nineteenth century it was still mainly the better off members of society, the upper and middle classes, who were able to take a holiday at the seaside. These people would usually 'take apartments' whereby they would rent two or more rooms and the landlady would cook the meals with the food the guests provided. In many cases servants came with their employers. One upper-middle class visitor to the town in 1899 was a Lieutenant-Colonel J W Bird whose four week stay lasted from 24 July until 23 August. On his return to London Lieutenant-Colonel Bird wrote a diary covering his holiday in Great Yarmouth, giving a picture of how a person of his 'class' passed his time on a holiday he described as 'very enjoyable'. Nothing is known about the background of the Birds or where they stayed in the town but the diary was printed privately, probably only for circulation among their friends. It is probable that the Lieutenant-Colonel had retired from army service otherwise he would have been serving in South Africa as this was at the height of the Boer War. As he had not visited the town before Lieutenant-Colonel Bird was somewhat dubious as to what the town was like and whether his health would benefit by a trip to the East Coast of England. He writes:

Monday 24 July:
I went down to Gt Yarmouth to look for apartments, and after some trouble succeeded in finding some facing the sea, the view from the house being very charming. In the afternoon I went up the Revolving Tower and as I understand machinery this gave me much pleasure as I considered it unique. I arrived back in town [London] *late and tired out, bringing some bloaters with me.*

Wednesday 26 July:
Mrs Bird and I left town for Yarmouth and reached our destination about a quarter to two where we found a very nice dinner (which I had ordered on the Monday) waiting for us. We went out to tea, after which we took a long walk.

ROYAL AQUARIUM
DINING ROOMS

NOW OPEN

THE NEW TERRACE SALOON,

On the East Side of the Building, facing the Sea.

REFRESHMENTS AT POPULAR PRICES.

The following served daily in the various Dining Rooms:—

The 2/- HOT DINNER,

Choice of Joints, with two kinds Vegetables, Bread, Cheese, Butter, Salad,
ad. lib.

THE

POPULAR 1/- DINNER,

Consisting of Hot Joints, two kinds Vegetables, Bread, Cheese. Served from 12.30
till 3 daily.

DITTO WITH PASTRY, 1/3.

The 1/- TEA,

Consisting of Tea, Bread and Butter, Cake, Shrimps, or Salad.
As much as you please.

The Marvellous 8d. TEA,

Consisting of Tea or Coffee, Bread and Butter, Cake, Shrimps or Water Cress, from
3 till 6.30.

Wedding Breakfasts, Dinners and Ball Suppers.

TRADE DINNERS PROVIDED.

Any number from 1 to 1,000 can be accommodated.

J. W. NIGHTINGALE, Lessee & Refreshment Contractor.

For particulars see Bills and Special Announcements

The Royal Aquarium dining rooms, run by Mr Nightingale, were popular with
visitors because of the reasonable prices and good quality food.

This picture of the Royal Aquarium was taken in the week commencing
2 October 1893. On the right the two lamp posts and railings are at the entrance to the
old Britannia Pier. When the pier was rebuilt in 1901 the entrance was moved further
to the east to give easier access to the new North Drive.

Thursday 27 July.
*We got up at 7.30am, had breakfast at 8.30am and went out. Mrs Bird
went up the tower and enjoyed the extensive panorama. Then we went
for a cruise in a yacht for about two hours. In the evening we went to
the theatre* [Theatre Royal] *to see 'The Liars' over which we both laughed
heartily.*

Friday 28 July.
*We went to Norwich by steamer and were very pleased with the trip up
the Broads. We did not have more than two hours in Norwich,
reaching Yarmouth at 8.30pm and shortly after we retired to rest.*

Saturday 29 July.
*Mrs Bird and I went to be photographed, after which we went for a
walk and returned to dinner. We had tea about 5 o'clock after which
we went to the theatre* [Royal Aquarium] *to see 'Gentleman Joe' and were
much amused. We returned to our apartments and retired to rest
shortly after half past eleven.*

Sunday 30 July.

We breakfasted early after which I wrote some letters. We went to St Nicholas church and came back to dinner at one o'clock. During the evening we went for a drive to see the Volunteer Encampment [on the South Denes] and upon our return went to the Pier to listen to the band.

Monday 31 July.

We went out early in the morning searching the town for medals and curios [which he collected]. We had tea at home and then went on the beach to a concert, which was rather amusing. We followed this with an oyster supper and returned home to bed about 11.

Tuesday 1 August.

Breakfast at 8 o'clock and then we went for a sail. After tea we went to a concert where we had 16 distinct turns for the small sum of two pence. We then returned home to a lobster supper after which we retired to rest.

Wednesday 2 August.

We went to Lowestoft, which is only 8 miles by sea. We did not think much of the place and after five hours returned to Yarmouth which we reached about seven o'clock.

Thursday 3 August.

This day was very uneventful but full of rest which we both needed very badly. We reached as far as the Pier and the day not being too hot we were able to sit out in the sun. After tea we went to a concert on the Pier and then returned home to supper.

Friday 4 August.

I had the misfortune to loose my gold folders [spectacles] which was very annoying. We went to a concert but were not very much taken by the performance.

Saturday 5 August.

Another quiet day. Quite unexpectedly my glasses turned up. In the evening we went to a concert.

Sunday 6 August.

We went to church as usual. So many excursionists and people arrived at Yarmouth yesterday that there was not sufficient house accommodation for them and many had to sleep under bathing machines or where they could. There was such a crush that we were unable to walk along the pavements and as we could not walk comfortably we returned home and went to bed early.

Monday 7 August.
Bank Holiday. We thought we would not venture on any excursion on account of the great number of people. We went for a ride in a motor carriage, which we much enjoyed.

RIVER AND RAIL

EXCURSION TRIPS
FROM
YARMOUTH to NORWICH
AND BACK DAILY,

(Sundays excepted). The Fine Saloon Screw Steamer

CITY OF NORWICH,

Built expressly for this Serpentine River, fitted throughout with Electric Light and every accommodation, the Saloon being Upholstered and most spacious, leaves

HALL QUAY, YARMOUTH,

At 10 a.m. Returning from Norwich 3.30 p.m.

Return Fare, 2/-. Single, 1/6.

Boat and Rail or Boat only.

Refreshments of first-class quality on board, and Tea supplied on Return Journey.

Tuesday 8 August.
Went for a two hour cruise in a sailing boat after which we dined out. In the evening we went to see 'The Belle of New York' [at the Royal Aquarium] but our enjoyment was partly spoilt as we had to wait outside the theatre for some considerable time in the crush, although we went to the early door and paid sixpence each extra. [It was customary to allow patrons to 'queue jump' by paying extra at a special door.]

Wednesday 9 August.
We both felt very seedy after yesterdays fun. Two sad thing happened today, a young man was drowned and one of a troupe of minstrels, having finished his turn, dropped down dead.

Thursday 10 August.
We left at quarter past nine for Cromer [by rail from Beach Station]. Mrs Bird and I thought it one of the most uninteresting towns we have ever been in.

Friday 11 August.
Rested all day and needed to do so after the long railway journey of the previous day.

Saturday 12 August.
We went to the photographers again and then to the market. After tea went to a concert on the beach, which was rather amusing.

The Revolving Tower stood north of the
Britannia Pier, the site today being a car
park. The toilets shown in front of the tower
still exist. At the base of the tower was a
small pavilion with refreshment rooms and a
few amusements. The tower opened on 19
June 1897 and was demolished in 1941.

Below is the Singers Ring or Chappell's
Ring on the Central Beach, later the site of
the open air Marina Theatre.

Sunday 13 August
We went to church in the morning.

Monday 14 August.
*We had a visitor. Mr F Bird's son and his friend called to see us. At half
past eleven we went to the market. After tea we went on the Pier and
then to a concert.*

Tuesday 15 August.
We visited the old church. The burial ground is not kept so well as I would like it to be.

Wednesday 16 August.
A quiet day spent walking about the front. There are always some horses on the rank, this I attribute to the charge of three shillings an hour.

Thursday 17 August.
We went for a sail. On board the yacht I met two funny fellows; one had grown old in the service of Lord George Sanger as a circus clown. In the summer he takes a partner to accompany him on the fiddle and sings comic songs. At the end of the season he intends to take a public house at Sheerness. After tea we went to a concert. One good point about Yarmouth is that there are two theatres and twenty concerts [an exaggeration] *so that one who is not satisfied with this would be hard to please.*

Friday 18 August.
A very dull day but the rain kept off. Paid a visit to the old Guild Hall and in the evening went to the Theatre Royal to see 'Don Quixote'.

Saturday 19 August.
We paid a visit to the old Toll House. [There follows a description of this 'interesting relic of antiquity'.]

Sunday 20 August.
We went as usual to St Nicholas church. After dinner we went for a stroll up and down the promenade, which is frequented by middle-class people and trippers who were very orderly. Rowdyism and bad behaviour is a thing unknown which I put down to free education.

Monday 21 August.
We went for a coach drive to Burgh Castle which we reached about twelve.

Tuesday 22 August.
This was a busy day as we had to do the packing. In the evening however we went for a short walk.

<u>Wednesday 23 August.</u>

Went to the market in the morning and dispatched some boxes of bloaters to my friends. We left Yarmouth shortly after two and reached London just after five. I am very pleased to say that we returned home very much better in health and quite delighted with Yarmouth and fully intend going there next year if we are spared.

A variety of horse transport near the Jetty waiting to take visitors on trips along the sea front or to country destinations such as Ormesby Eels Foot.

Piers and Entertainment

Seaside piers, originally designed as landing stages for steamers, quickly became fashionable as promenades in Victorian times, attractions no large resort could afford to be without. At Great Yarmouth the Wellington Pier opened in 1853, the first new pier to be built in the country for eleven years and the first to be built solely for pleasure purposes and not as a landing stage. A pier had first been suggested in 1843 but it was not until 1852, the year the Duke of Wellington died that suggestions that a pier be built as a memorial to the Duke received local support. A company was formed, the necessary Act obtained and the first pile driven on 28 June 1853. Work progressed well and by November 550 feet of pier were opened to the public, the complete 700 feet being finished in May the following year, the total cost £6,776. Entertainment on the pier was provided by military bands, mainly the band of the East Norfolk Militia and from 1891 Variety Concerts took place twice daily in a small building at the eastern end.

In 1899 the original company was in financial difficulty and sold the pier to the Corporation which laid out gardens on the south side, complete with bandstand, and constructed a pavilion at the end of the pier which opened 13 July 1903. The first variety show in the new pavilion included singers, comedians, Professor Garford with his dogs and pigeons and Bert Woodward, advertised as 'a cycling coon'. A Winter Garden was bought from Torquay and re-erected on the northern side of the pier entrance, opening in June 1904. The new Winter Garden proved very popular and in 1907 roller skating was introduced. Shortly after this an outside track for speed roller skating was built in the gardens and military bands again became a popular attraction in the bandstand. In 1928 a new frontage for the pier complex was erected, designed to match the pavilion.

From 1949 Catlins Showtime was the main summer show with a variety of 'big names' appearing at the Sunday concerts. In 1957 Bernard Delfont took over the summer show with Benny Hill in 'Light up the Town'. The Delfont shows ran for several years and attracted many top name television stars to the town. It was not uncommon for over 10,000 people to see the show each week at the height of the summer season and this format continued until the late 1970's. In the 1980's the fortunes of the Wellington Pier declined as a succession of

This engraving shows the scene when the first pile of the Wellington Pier was driven on 28 June 1853 by the Mayor Samuel Marsh.

The original entrance to the Wellington Pier which opened 1 May 1854. The single storey building seen at the end of the pier was erected in 1883. For many years the band of the East Norfolk Militia provided the entertainment on the pier but from 1891 Variety Concerts were introduced in addition to the Military Bands.

The new pavilion under construction early in 1903. The opening night was 13 July that year with a variety show. The pavilion cost £3000 and was built in twelve weeks.

business men took over and at one point the Corporation considered demolition as the answer to the failing pier. In 1995 the comedian Jim Davidson was given a 25 year rent free deal to try and transform the pier. In 1954 a part of the gardens known as the south lawn was turned into Pixieland which in 1961 became the Merrivale Model Village. In 1966 the Winter Garden became the Biergarten and eventually the roller skating ceased as it turned into a night club.

So popular had been the town's first pier that in July 1858 another, the Britannia, was opened. The Act for building this pier was obtained in 1857 and included clauses that no shops or buildings other than bathing, reading or refreshment rooms were to be built on the pier, the only exception being a tollhouse and a lighthouse. The pier was built in line with Regent Road and the entrance was in line with the eastern side of the Aquarium. At the entrance were two small buildings between which were ornate gates, on the south side but under the pier was a public house known as Uncle Toms Cabin, the access being from the beach. The following year the first of a series of disasters befell this pier when a schooner, driven by a gale, cut the pier in two, the rebuilt pier being shorter by 80 feet. From 1867 the pier was used as a landing stage for the daily London to Yarmouth passenger boat service and in 1868 another schooner, the *Seagull*, sliced through the pier taking away 100 feet. On an open stage at the eastern end of the pier Dunn's Concert Party entertained from 1878.

At the end of the 1900 season the Britannia Pier was demolished and a new one, 810 feet long, built to replace it. The New Britannia Pier opened on 21 June 1902 with a grand pavilion seating 1200 people at the eastern end. Shops were included in the new development and a feature of the pier at this time was the Penny on the Mat ride. In December 1909 disaster struck again when fire completely destroyed the pavilion. Rebuilding began almost immediately, a new pavilion being ready for the following season. Five years later this was also destroyed by fire, this time the fire attributed to (but not proven) members of the Suffragette movement who had been refused permission to hold a meeting there. Rebuilt for the second time a new pavilion opened the following July. In 1932 the Floral Hall Ballroom on the pier was destroyed by fire and in the Second World War a section of the pier was blown up to prevent any possible use as a landing point during an invasion. In 1954 the pavilion was once again burnt down together with the Ocean Ballroom and Bar. The present pavilion opened in June 1958 and in 1967 a new entrance to the pier was built, this included what was to be the first escalator in the town. Variety and Pierrot shows were the main forms of entertainment in the Pavilion until 1946 when Tom Arnold took over as producer of the summer show and from 1950 'big name' shows began with Frankie Howerd. Other entertainment facilities were now built on the pier and the summer shows have continued to the present day.

Reg Maddox's Evening Follies was the resident company at the Wellington Pier for the 1929 season, a season which ran from 18 May to 5 October.

The old Britannia Pier in the 1890's

One of the earliest forms of entertainment at the seaside was provided by groups known as Nigger Minstrels, performing in 'rings', round boarded enclosures with a small platform for a stage at one side. On the north Yarmouth beach there was a Nigger Minstrel Ring opposite Norfolk Square. This opened in July 1897 and as this was Jubilee year it is not surprising it was named the Diamond Jubilee Minstrel Ring. It had a capacity of 2000 and shows were given at 11am, 3pm and 7pm each day. The wooden structure was dismantled after each season and stored in a warehouse in St Nicholas Road. The last season for this ring was 1909 and two years later the warehouse and its contents were destroyed by fire.

On the south beach opposite Goode's Hotel a similar ring had opened in 1881. Towards the end of the century Nigger Minstrel groups had been replaced by concert parties which adopted the name Pierrots. The ring on the south beach became known as Chappell's Ring after James Chappell who took over the lease from 1884 and from 1919 Frank Gee's Troubadours were the resident entertainers for many years. This concert ring survived until 1934 when it was demolished to make way for the new open air Marina theatre which opened in 1937.

The Pavilion under construction on the New Britannia Pier April 1902.

The Pavilion Promenade on the New Britannia Pier June 1902.

The temporary building erected on the Britannia Pier for Dunn's Concert Party
before the permanent pavilion was built. This picture taken 5 September 1901.

BRITANNIA PIER & PAVILION,

Managing Director]   **GT. YARMOUTH.**   [Mr J. W. NIGHTINGALE.

ONE NIGHT ONLY!
Wednesday, Sept. 20th, at 8 p.m.,

MRS. LANGTRY
- IN -

"MY MILLINER'S BILL,"

Assisted by

COMPANY OF STAR ARTISTES.

**1st Reserved Seats, 3/-.   2nd Reserved Seats, 2/-.   3rd Seats, 1/6.
Body of Hall & Balcony Seats, 1/-. Promenade & Back Seats, 6d.**

1st & 2nd Reserved Seats can now be Booked at Pier Entrance. No Pier Admission will be
charged on Seats Booked in Advance.

JARROLD & SONS, LTD., PRINTERS, GT. YARMOUTH.

One of Lilly Langtry's appearances at Great Yarmouth 20 September 1905.

Other entertainment in the town included the famous Christy's Minstrels who appeared at the Corn Exchange as early as 1860. In addition to playing at the 'rings' the Concert Parties entertained on the piers, after the turn of the century using the new pavilions. From these shows the tradition of seaside entertainment became established. On the beach one the earliest forms of entertainment was the Punch and Judy show, the first in the town being Knox & King's Punch and Judy in 1907. The camera obscura was another popular beach attraction as were the beach entertainers such as palmists, phrenologists and musicians while a variety of vendors sold everything from ice cream to monkey nuts. The beach photographer with his portable dark room and tripod camera appeared in the 1880's, replaced in the twentieth century by Jackson's Faces and other photographers along the promenade.

Moving pictures had first been seen at fairgrounds in the 1890's and in March 1897 'Living Photographs' were shown at the Liberal Club Assembly Rooms in the Market Place. This building was later to be known as the Bijou Hall, demolished to 1914 to make way for the Central Cinema, today the site of Woolworth's store. Moving films were a rival entertainment to the minstrels and concert parties and soon they were being shown at many venues including the Theatre Royal, the pier pavilions, the Royal Aquarium, the Hippodrome and a small building at the base of the Revolving Tower.

The Gem on the Marine Parade was the first purpose-built cinema in the town, opening in July 1908 and advertising 'a continuous flow of Electric Vaudeville showing all day long'. Films continued at the Gem until it closed in 1939. When it was reopened in 1946 by Jack Jay the name had changed to the Windmill and live shows replaced the films for the summer seasons. The Yarmouth Follies of 1948 starred the radio comedians Dan & Jim Sherry and in 1955 Tommy Trinder made his first of many appearances at the theatre. Other big names to appear at the Windmill included Tommy Steele, Frankie Howerd, Billy Fury and Joe Brown. In 1962 Allan Smethurst the Singing Postman appeared there in a summer show. Bingo was now played at the Windmill during the winter months. In the 1980's the summer shows finished and the Windmill became a children's fun house known as Wally's Windmill followed in 1992 by the Ripleys Believe it or Not exhibition. In 1998 it became a Waxworks and in 2001 it opened as an indoor Adventure Golf.

The second Britannia Pier Pavilion which opened in 1910 and was destroyed
by fire on 17 April 1914

The popularity of films led to the Empire Picture Playhouse
opening in 1911 and films were shown here until 1991 when it became
a Bingo Hall and in 1996 a theme bar, Bourbon Street. The Regent
Variety and Picture Palace in Regent Road opened on Boxing Day 1914,
one of the most elaborate cinema buildings in the country. It was here in
1929 the first talking film was shown in the town, a film called *Weary
River* starring Richard Barthelemess. Although occasional live shows
were produced here the Regent continued to show films until it closed in
1982, reopening as a bingo hall two years later. At the western end of
Regent Road the Regal cinema opened in 1934 and from 1948 presented
summer variety shows changing to a resident summer show in 1959.
During the winter months the Regal, later known as the ABC, reverted
to a cinema. As with the other summer shows many 'big name' stars
appeared here both for the season and at the Sunday concerts, names
which included the Beatles and the Irish group the Batchelors. From
1987 the ABC became known as the Cannon, before it was closed and
later demolished.

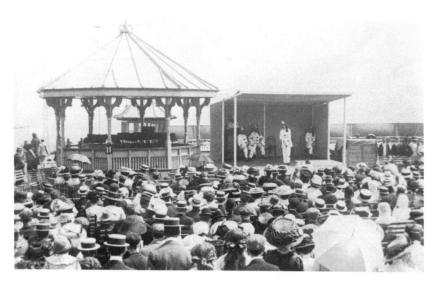

Adeler & Sutton's Pierrots who appeared twice daily on the deck of the Britannia Pier in July and August 1906, the first open air pierrot show in the town.

The Windmill summer show for 1980 *Further Confessions of a Window Cleaner* starring Robin Askwith. Local window cleaners were invited to a special reception on 5 June. A sharp contrast to the 1906 entertainment above.

40

Gorleston-on-Sea

Towards the end of the nineteenth century the small fishing village of Gorleston began to develop as a holiday resort, offering an alternative type of holiday to its larger neighbour Great Yarmouth which at that time was experiencing a rapid growth in amusements and entertainment. In 1889 a sea wall was built at the foot of the Gorleston cliffs and the Great Yarmouth Council announced a set of regulations covering the beach, cliffs and Parade. No person was allowed to walk or lie on the cliff slope, begging, hawking, puppet shows and dangerous or noisy games were banned. The old public house favoured by the beachmen and fishermen, the Anchor & Hope at the foot of the south pier, was replaced by a new hotel and renamed the Pier. At the same time many private houses in the Cliff Hill area began to open their doors as apartments and lodging houses to the increasing number of summer visitors. In 1896 the Beach Gardens, complete with bandstand, were laid out in front of the Pier Hotel and a wooden promenade was constructed between the gardens and the beach. In 1898 two houses on the cliff top overlooking the harbour entrance were extended and altered to form a large new hotel, appropriately named the Cliff Hotel, designed by the Norwich architect George Skipper. An arched entrance and a flight of steps led up from the beach with shelters, pavilion and tennis courts on the top of the cliff. The hotel had 139 bedrooms and its pepper-pot towers gave it a distinctive appearance. A serious fire on Boxing Day 1915 destroyed much of the original hotel, the surviving portion forming part of the present day Cliff Hotel.

Entertainment for early holiday makers was provided by concerts held twice a week in the Tramway Hotel concert room or outside in their Pleasure Gardens. In 1879 the Tramway was advertising its Pleasure Ground, Bowling Green and Quoit Ground with 'Grand Galas every Monday and Thursday during the season'. Admission was 3d, or 4d including a tram ticket. The Tramway Hotel was destroyed in the Second World War and later rebuilt on the same site. In 1884 Lenton's Concert Party appeared at Gorleston on Bank Holiday Monday and in 1903 the Court Comedy Pierrots performed in the Cliff Hill Gardens, opposite the White Lion Hotel, an hotel which had been rebuilt and enlarged in 1897. In 1904 Uncle Walter's Pierrots, a group of five entertainers, performed on the cliffs. On the quay, opposite the landing stage for the

Elsie & Doris Waters Enthusiasts 1927

The Pavilion Show August 1901

The Pavilion 1938. The main entrance was originally on the west side of the
building as seen here.

The Beach Gardens and Bandstand c1910, long before the Floral Hall and swimming pool were built. Beside the Pavilion the small building with the large open doors is the Rocket House where life saving apparatus was kept.

Belle steamers was a piece of land known as the Quay Gardens and here the Varsity Pierrot & Concert Party began in 1911. By 1914 a building had been erected on the site and was known as the Olympia Alfresco Pavilion but the outbreak of war on 5 August that year brought this and all other entertainment venues to a close.

The Gorleston Pavilion was the first effort by the Corporation to enter the field of indoor entertainment and is today the second oldest entertainment building in the Borough. It opened in July 1900 with little publicity, probably because the building was not complete. Unglazed windows and insufficient seating meant the variety show had a difficult first night, particularly as a band played continuously in the adjacent Beach Gardens. The situation had improved when the 1901 season opened on 8 July, the building was complete. In its early days the Pavilion provided day long entertainment in two halls. In the large hall there were sessions at 11am, 3pm, 4.30pm and 7pm while in the smaller hall they were timed at 12.15am, 3.30pm and 5.30pm so that shows ran in conjunction, giving continuous entertainment. In addition to these shows there were Sunday Concerts at 3.30pm and 8.15pm. In 1908 George Gilbert, owner of the Yarmouth Hippodrome, became the lessee and he changed the name to the Palace for the next five years. The building was now used mainly as a cinema but there were occasional variety shows. It once again became the Pavilion in

1913 when Henry Clay's Musical Party opened. The Pavilion was to be the centre of entertainment in Gorleston for many years and the tea rooms, lounge and balcony overlooking the gardens were popular for lunch, tea and supper. Elsie and Doris Waters, later to become the well known radio and music hall duo Gert and Daisie, took the lease in 1927 for their show 'The Enthusiasts' and in 1928 the Gorleston Gossips Concert Party played there. It was at the Pavilion that Bill Pertwee, later better known for his role in 'Dads Army', started his concert party days in 1955. Throughout the 1950's the Pavilion lost money in competition with the large shows in Great Yarmouth. A new type of show had to be found and it was decided to remove all the fixed seating in favour of tables and chairs and try an Olde Tyme Music Hall which opened on 24 June 1963. All seats were priced at 3s (15p) and during its 13 week season the show had an 89% capacity audience. The Music Hall format has been a successful feature of the Pavilion shows ever since.

In a guide book for 1904 Gorleston was described as a village and a 'delightful holiday resort'. The Corporation had made a considerable investment in Gorleston the previous year in extending the Marine Parade, erecting shelters and making a Ravine cut through the cliffs, with a bridge over it, as a new approach to the beach. This led to new development along the cliffs, away from the old village. The cliff walks and shelters, safe beach and bathing, gardens and bandstand were the main attractions together with the lifeboat house and the Pavilion. The Cliff Hotel was said to 'give the village a thoroughly up-to-date appearance'. A proposal to erect a Singers Ring on the beach was abandoned due to local opposition. In 1903 the new coastal rail link between Lowestoft and Yarmouth passed through Gorleston, a station being built in a cutting off Victoria Road and another, Gorleston North, off Burgh Road. Access to the fast emerging new resort was now available by tram, train and steamer. In 1905 the horse tram system, which had linked Yarmouth and Gorleston from the west side of the Haven Bridge for thirty years, was replaced by a new electric tramway.

In July 1924 the New Beach Gardens were opened to replace those first set out in 1896. Many concert parties entertained in these gardens, Jack Hylton the well known band leader started his career as a pianist at one of these shows. The centrepiece of the new gardens was a bandstand which had previously stood outside the Hippodrome

This postcard shows late Edwardian holiday makers enjoying the beach at
Gorleston in 1908. A few bathing machines are in evidence but most people
appear to prefer paddling.

The White Lion steps c1910. Behind the bushes on the right is Duncan's Well, a well
sunk in 1797 on the orders of Admiral Lord Duncan to supply water to the Naval fleet
during the Napoleonic Wars.

on Yarmouth sea front. Built in 1912 this had not been used as a bandstand at Yarmouth but as a vivarium or snake pit. Up to 60 reptiles including snakes, lizards and baby crocodiles were kept in a pit while a gentleman known as Oscar demonstrated how to handle them in safety. When re-erected at Gorleston Military Bands replaced the reptiles.

In 1919 Henry Clay, who had earlier produced variety shows at the Pavilion, leased a meadow near the William IV public house and erected a marquee for his Gorleston Pops concert party. In 1925 the marquee was replaced by a wooden Concert Hall which was in use until demolished in 1934. In the 1950's the meadow was used as a Pitch & Putt Course and is today used for children's amusements but it is still known as Pops Meadow.

Although the Gorleston beach was not as commercialised as Great Yarmouth there were bathing machines from the 1890's. Many of these were owned by the Capps family who ran 13 single machines and four family machines. Swimming lessons were also available as were changing tents and refreshments.

In 1926 a Model Yacht Pond and Paddling Pool were constructed. The following year the Palace cinema in Beach Road, which had opened in 1913 as Filmland, provided live entertainment with concert parties. The other Gorleston cinema, the Coliseum in the High Street, continued to show films. In 1939 the original Palace cinema closed and the New Palace opened in the High Street. This was converted to a Bingo Hall in 1964 and the Coliseum demolished in 1970, ending over fifty years of cinema in Gorleston.

In May 1937 the Gorleston Super Holiday Camp opened, advertised as the 'Queen Mary of Holiday Camps', the same year that Billy Butlin opened his first camp at Skegness. Founded by a London businessman Mr Charles Haigh the camp was built at a cost of £50,000 and soon became a popular new addition to the town. Only two seasons later the camp was forced to close for the duration of the war during which time it was used to accommodate troops. It reopened in 1946 and finally closed in 1973. Two years later the buildings, which comprised brick chalets, a ballroom and dining hall were demolished and the houses of Elmhurst Court built on the site. During the 1953 East Coast floods many people who were evacuated from houses in Southtown and Cobholm were accommodated at the camp, some for several weeks.

Punch & Judy on Gorleston beach in 1937

MATTHES' ASSEMBLY ROOMS
ENGLAND'S LANE, GORLESTON-ON-SEA.

We undertake Catering of every description and respectfully solicit the privilege of submitting estimates and quotations for EVERY BRANCH OF CATERING.

FISHING, BOATING, AND PRIVATE DINNER PARTIES, OUTINGS AND BEANFEASTS, TEAS, ETC.

Contractors for supplying Marquees, Tents, and all Camp Equipment, Chairs and Tabling, Cutlery, etc.

MATTHES' ASSEMBLY ROOMS.
Accommodation for 130 Persons.

Terms and Quotations from :
L. MATTHES,
Caterers and Confectioners,
Gorleston-on-Sea.

Head Office, Works, and Catering Dept. :
ENGLAND'S LANE.

Telephone : 20 Gorleston
Telegraphic Address :
"Matthes, Phone,
Great Yarmouth."

Branches :
HIGH STREET.
BELL'S ROAD.
AND AT
179, LONDON ROAD,
LOWESTOFT.

SEASON BRANCHES :
BRITANNIA PIER TEAROOMS, GREAT YARMOUTH
(Accommodation can be made for Parties up to 750 Persons) ;
SPARROWS NEST TEAROOMS and NORTH DENES RECREATION GROUNDS, LOWESTOFT.

Matthes Assembly Rooms in Englands Lane was a popular venue for many events in pre-war Gorleston. This advertisement is from a 1928 Holiday Guide.

The Beach Gardens were replaced in 1939 by a new complex consisting of a dance hall complete with sun lounge and an open air swimming pool. The new dance hall was named the Floral Hall and bandleaders such as Eddie Gates, Bert Galey and Gordon Edwards provided the dance music for many years. The dance hall has remained, now known as the Ocean Rooms, but the swimming pool was demolished after much controversy and local opposition in 1993, gardens once again laid out on the site.

A 1948 guide describes Gorleston as:

"far removed from the stress and turmoil of city life - a haven where you can live under the happiest of conditions."

To this day Gorleston has remained a quiet alternative to Great Yarmouth and has resisted large scale holiday developments. As with other seaside resorts it has seen a decline in popularity and many hotels and guest houses have changed to residential homes but the Pavilion has maintained its popularity, used for many amateur productions as well as the regular summer shows.

The main entrance building at Gorleston Holiday Camp 1937-1973

The Bass Outings

There have been many organised works outings to Great Yarmouth over the years from all parts of the country but the largest and most meticulously organised were those by the Burton-on-Trent brewery of Bass, Ratcliff & Gretton. From the 1860's the railway network had enabled many companies to organise works outings which fulfilled several purposes, they educated the workers, kept employees happy and contented and were an important source of advertising for the company. The Bass brewery organised their first trip in 1865 and by 1883 it had become an annual event eagerly awaited by all employees. In common with Victorian principles each social group of the workforce was firmly segregated, both on the journey and at the destination. Every employee was given their usual days pay and in addition a gratuity of half-a-crown ($12^1/_2$p) to cover refreshments during the day. Those employed in the office received 5/- (25p) and a first-class seat on the train. From 1890 the annual excursions alternated between Scarborough, Blackpool, Liverpool and Great Yarmouth.

The first excursion to Yarmouth was on Friday 16 June 1893, a day when fifteen special trains brought a total of 8,000 Bass employees and their families for a day at the seaside, the group including about 500 children. The organiser for Bass was William Walters, the company Traffic Manager and on his behalf the Yarmouth end was organised by the local entrepreneur and owner of the Royal Aquarium John Nightingale. Nothing was left to chance and every detail of the excursion was carefully planned. Every employee was given a detailed programme of arrangements and the latest copy of 'The Popular Guide to Yarmouth' complete with map.

The first train left Burton at 3.50am and arrived at Yarmouth Vauxhall at 8.30am. On the way a ten minute stop (on later excursions this was reduced to eight minutes) was made at Peterborough where passengers could alight for refreshments, stalls being set out along the length of the platform. A cup of tea with a slice of bread and butter cost 2d, a sandwich 2d and a pork pie 4d. The remaining trains left Burton at ten minute intervals and the last train reached Yarmouth at 10.50am. Such was the railway organisation that the trains maintained the ten minute interval between them for the duration of the journey. For the first part of the journey to March the complete route was closed for all

Above: Bass workers in their Sunday best and with their families alight from one of the trains at Yarmouth Vauxhall station for the 1909 outing. As usual the occasion was recorded by the company photographer Mr Simnett.

Left: The free pass issued to all workers for the 1913 outing. On earlier outings the rail ticket was the free pass.

The Pay Office and entrance gates to the New Britannia Pier when it reopened in 1902. Bass excursionists were given free access to the pier and pavilion.

Uncle Tom's Cabin at the entrance to the old Britannia Pier. The entrance to this public house was discretely placed on the beach, from the pier deck the building was the Refreshment Rooms. A severe storm and high tide in 1883 wrecked the Cabin but it was rebuilt and remained until the old pier was demolished in 1900. No doubt many Bass workers on the earlier excursions found their way into Uncle Tom's at some time during the day.

other rail traffic except the Bass excursion trains. Midland Railway engines pulled the trains as far as Peterborough where they were changed for engines of the Great Eastern Railway. The 182 mile journey took $4\frac{1}{2}$ hours and at Yarmouth two miles of sidings were required to stable the 250 coaches. The return journey commenced at 7.30pm, the last train leaving Vauxhall at 9.50pm and arriving back at Burton at 2.35am. In addition to the trains from Burton a special excursion train brought staff from the London office into Southtown station. Seats were allocated on each train to a particular group of workers and it was stressed that it was imperative that all persons travelled on their allocated train, both for the outward and for the return journey. In the programme Mr Walters wrote:

> *"may I especially beg of all persons to be quiet and orderly on the journey, on the Steamers, at the various places of amusement, in the streets and generally throughout the day. It should be remembered that this is our first visit to Yarmouth: let it be said therefore that Bass & Co's employees knew how to behave themselves, and that all returned home perfectly orderly and sober."*

The last request may have been too much to expect from a brewery outing but he also asked:

> *"none of the men should throw empty bottles etc. out of the carriage windows, especially while the train is in motion as such proceedings are highly dangerous to the platelayers and others employed on the railway."*

It should be noted that most of the train was made up with non corridor carriages, a fact that could have accounted for an excessive number of discarded bottles. The train ticket was the most important item the excursionists had, it was described as their 'open sesame' for all the places of entertainment as arrangements for free admission had been arranged to any ticket holder throughout the day.

An electric tram, a horse brake and a horse bus pass each other outside
the Bath Hotel c1910.

The Barking Smack and the Marine public houses. The forecourt of the Marine was
well known for the oyster stalls. Between the buildings can be seen Ellis's Restaurant
on the corner of St Peters Road and Wellington Road.

One of the port steam tugs the *Lord Nelson* which in the summer months was used as a pleasure boat and plied daily between Yarmouth and Lowestoft, seen here in 1904. The tug was built in 1899 and broken up in 1919. For the Bass excursions this was hired for their exclusive use.

It was stated in the programme:

> *"the whole of Yarmouth has been practically secured for the benefit of a day's enjoyment for Bass work people and their wives and children."*

Mr Walters made his headquarters at the Royal Hotel (which was owned by Nightingale) where anyone with a problem could go for advice or help. Places like the Royal Aquarium, Theatre Royal, the Piers and Parish Church all had special events or concerts while all places of historical interest in the town were open. Boat trips both out to sea and on the river were available as were tennis courts, bathing machines and donkey rides. Military displays, fireworks displays and band concerts were arranged and all outside entertainment had an alternative venue if the weather was inclement.

Horse brakes were available for trips into the surrounding countryside to such places as Ormesby Broad, Winterton Lighthouse, Belton Gardens and Fritton. The Theatre Royal provided entertainment suitable for the women and children such as a Pantomime while the Switchback Railway and the Hotchkiss Bicycle Railway could expect at least 6,000 customers each during the day. Twenty donkeys were at the disposal of the women and children, each donkey distinguished by a coloured rosette. For those intent on a dip in the sea bathing machines were reserved for both ladies and gentlemen from 9am until 2pm, each machine identified by a label 'Bass & Co.' Costumes, drawers and towels were also supplied.

The Royal Aquarium was at this period divided into two departments, the Refreshment Department and the Theatre. Any number from 1 to 1000 could be accommodated in the various dining rooms and another 400 in the Minor Hall. Prices for a meal varied from 1/- to £1. In the First Class Dining Room an 'à la Carte' menu was available as well as a 2/- (10p) dinner, this consisting of hot joints, vegetables, bread, butter and cheese. A cold lunch was available for 1/9 and for tea there was bread, butter, cake, shrimps, salad and preserves for 1/- (5p). This catering was provided by Mr Nightingale who also arranged a stall selling kippers and bloaters for the excursionists to take home at the end of the day.

One of the 'Belle' fleet of paddle steamers, the *Walton Belle*, was used to take Bass excursionists on sea trips. Seen here in 1904 proceeding up river stern first this boat was renamed the *Essex Queen* in 1924. The Belle steamers continued to operate a regular service from Yarmouth to London until the 1930's.

The beach and Jetty in the early 1900's. While the horse carriages await passengers the majority of people, and the tea stalls, are gathered near the high water mark. A large group are watching some form of beach entertainment. Note the crowded Jetty and that no one is sunbathing.

So successful was the first outing to Yarmouth that others followed at four yearly intervals.

1897 June 11	15 trains with 8,500 people
1901 June 14	16 trains with 10,000 people
1905 July 14	16 trains with 8,000 people
1909 July 23	15 trains with 9,000 people
1913 July 25	14 trains with 7,000 people

On each visit the Bass excursionists saw a different Yarmouth as the resort changed and new amenities were built. The 1905 visitors had the pleasure of two rebuilt piers complete with pavilions while those coming in 1909 found a new and imposing entertainment hall, the Gem, on the Marine Parade, described in the programme as an 'Animated Picture Hall'. By 1913 the Empire had been built and the new 'Waterplane Station' (the South Denes air station) was mentioned in the programme. Unknown to the excursionists this was to be their last visit to Yarmouth, the outbreak of war the following year led to the suspension of all such outings and for many reasons they were never resumed when peace returned. Bass justifiably claimed that their excursions were "the largest outings in the world".

Into the Twentieth Century

At the beginning of the century a holiday for many people meant a loss of earnings and the possible loss of a job. Annual holidays with pay were still some years away so it was only a small section of the population who were able to spend any length of time at the seaside. Many of the large private houses towards the eastern end of Regent Road and other roads leading to the sea front were now available as apartments or boarding houses. Typical of these was the Pier View Boarding Establishment at 50/51 Regent Road which in 1908 advertised 'late dinners, liberal table, nothing but the best English meat used. Perfect sanitation, billiard and smoke room, cycle accommodation for inclusive terms of 5/- (25p) per day.'

Great Yarmouth, as a seaside town, was increasing in popularity and private investment along the Marine Parade was ahead of Corporation investment. The town now had two rebuilt or refurbished piers and in 1902 the first shops appeared on the Marine Parade with the building of the Marine Arcade on the site of Ansell Place. Two years later a further arcade was added and now there were shops as diverse as a jeweller, tobacconist, toy shop, chemist, fruiterer, optician and Palmer Bros. fancy drapery shop. Today these shopping arcades have turned into the Leisureland amusement arcades.

On 19 June 1902 an electric tram service began in the town, among the first routes being Vauxhall Station to the Wellington Pier and Newtown to the Wellington Pier. A serious fire the previous year had destroyed Winton's Rooms next to the Coastguard Station on the Marine Parade together with the adjacent Jubilee Exhibition of Barron's. The amusements were quickly rebuilt and reopened as the Paradium, while in 1902 a new Goode's Hotel and Ballroom replaced Winton's Rooms, a building which was to be one of the main features of the Marine Parade for many years. Today this is Caesar's Palace amusement arcade. In 1903 George Gilbert's Hippodrome Circus opened, replacing a smaller wooden circus building on the same site, which had been in use since 1898. The new circus featured a sinking ring which held 60,000 gallons of water enabling the shows to include a 'water spectacular' a popular and unique feature which is still part of the Hippodrome circus today, much of the original equipment still being in use.

This aerial view from the top of the Revolving Tower c1910, probably taken on a Bank Holiday, shows in the foreground the New Britannia Pier and a congested Central Beach with the many stalls and entertainments on the beach. In the background can be seen the Singers Ring.

The Hippodrome Circus, seen here in the 1950's, was erected in 1903 by George Gilbert. Part of the Bath Hotel, on the left, had been purchased by Gilbert and demolished to provide this forecourt to enable the Hippodrome to be seen from the Marine Parade. On this forecourt stood the Vivarium or Snake Pit which was later moved to Gorleston to become a Bandstand.

The London boats at Hall Quay with the *Southend Belle* and the *Walton Belle* waiting to depart. Passengers for London had to change boats at Clacton on a trip which took up to twelve hours.

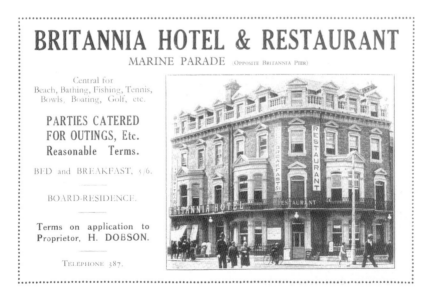

BRITANNIA HOTEL & RESTAURANT

MARINE PARADE (Opposite Britannia Pier)

Central for
Beach, Bathing, Fishing, Tennis,
Bowls, Boating, Golf, etc.

PARTIES CATERED
FOR OUTINGS, Etc.
Reasonable Terms.

BED and BREAKFAST, 5/6.

BOARD-RESIDENCE.

Terms on application to
Proprietor, H. DOBSON.

TELEPHONE 387.

The Britannia Hotel on the corner of Regent Road, 1931. This later became Hazell's Restaurant then a Waxworks and is today the Regent Food Court.

At the southern end of the Marine Parade the Nelson Gardens, model yacht pond and bowling greens opened in 1906, the first bowling greens on the sea front. In 1923 the gardens were rebuilt and the yacht pond, being little used, was enlarged and used for paddle boats. In 1927 another pond was constructed and the two linked by an ornamental bridge. In recent years the paddle boats have gone and the ponds now form part of the Pleasure Beach complex.

In 1909 a site on the beach was leased to the Great Yarmouth Beach Amusements Ltd. for a Scenic Railway and two side shows. A condition of the lease was that there were to be 'no steam organs, bands of music, sirens or other noisy instruments, refreshment stalls or automatic machines on the site'. The Scenic Railway and the Katzen Jammer Castle (a type of Fun House) opened on 24 July. The following year the River Caves under the scenic railway opened and these were followed by a Joy Wheel to replace the Castle. In 1912 remodelling with plaster mountains complete with snow capped peaks produced the Royal Mountain Scenic Railway which was in use until destroyed by fire in April 1919. Quickly rebuilt it reopened in August that year and in 1928 the lease was granted to Pat Collins and for the first time the site was known as the Pleasure Beach. By now there were many additional rides and side shows and in 1932 a new Rollercoaster, built in Germany in 1929 for the Colonial Exhibition, was shipped to the town to replace the old Scenic Railway. Built entirely of wood this is still one of the main attraction at the Pleasure Beach, East Anglia's most popular tourist attraction. Botton Brothers took over the Pleasure Beach in 1954 and in 1959 a new entrance was built, leading into a site which today covers nine acres and has 70 rides and attractions. The Giant Slide was added in the 1960's and a Water Chute built in 1972.

In 1910 the North Parade was extended north of Sandown Road while on the Marine Parade the Gem was equipped with a full size stage and handsome balcony. Barron's Picture Palace gained a cinematograph licence, now having seating for 300 persons. Donkey rides and goat carriages had for many years been an attraction at the seaside but in 1911 it was decided by the Council to withdraw all licenses for the goat carriages. By 1914 the town guide was advertising the recently constructed Royal Naval Air Station on the South Denes as an attraction, 'a centre of very great interest where aeroplanes and seaplanes can be seen flying almost daily'.

The shop of Ernest William Watts at 36 St Peters Road on the corner with Napoleon Place, Hairdresser and Tobacconist in 1908. The large sign, clearly visible from the Marine Parade, shows that sea water baths were still available in the twentieth century.

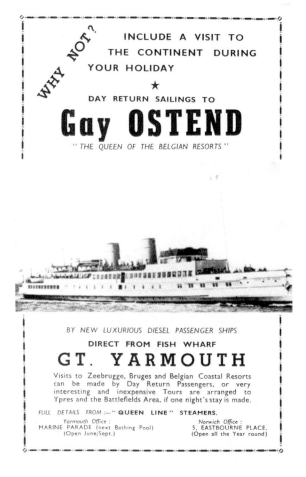
The first char-a-banc's ran an hourly service from Yarmouth to Lowestoft and on Bank Holiday Monday 1914 over 20,000 tickets were issued for Yarmouth trains from London and 10,000 from Norwich. Shortly after the Bank Holiday there was a declaration of war, the summer season was cut short and despite efforts to reassure people that there was no danger on the East Coast many people left the resort and others cancelled their holidays. The threat of German Naval vessels shelling coastal towns was enough to deter all but the most determined holiday maker and for the next four years the town offered limited facilities to only a few visitors, the town suffering a considerable financial loss.

The end of the Great War heralded a new era in seaside holidays. Men returned home from service overseas and were now not content with their previous lives, they wanted better wages, better houses, better food and holidays. In 1919 many families were to enjoy their first ever holiday and the Bank Holiday saw 50,000 excursionists in the town, many with nowhere to sleep except under the piers or bathing machines.

The Troubadours restarted their Variety Concerts on the Central Beach and the first Daily Express children's playground opened opposite the Marine Arcade where parents could leave children to play in safety, looked after by trained staff and a qualified nurse. Apartments were giving way to guest houses and Bed & Breakfast signs appeared in many windows as the 'seaside landlady' emerged. Coronation House on Marine Parade North was a typical Guest House, offering terms of $3\frac{1}{2}$ to $4\frac{1}{2}$ guineas per week. A bed at the Savoy Hotel in Regent Road, 'the largest and most central Temperance Hotel' was available for 4/- (20p) per night. These prices remained almost constant throughout the inter war years and this was also a period when more amusement arcades and family entertainment appeared. The Pierrot shows, exclusive to the seaside, were having their heyday.

On the Yarmouth beach in 1920 there were 28 refreshment stalls, 12 sites for bathing machines and tents, 13 photographers stands, 12 sites for motor boats, a donkey stand, four scale stands, a phrenologist, a sand modeller, a Punch & Judy and two shell fish stalls. In 1922 an open air swimming pool 100 yards long and 25 yards wide complete with diving platforms and water chute opened on the Marine Parade. Admission to this sea-water pool was 6d ($2\frac{1}{2}$p) for adults and galas and water frolics were held regularly throughout the season. The pool was demolished in 1979 shortly before the Marina Centre was built.

The Char-a -Banc Prince of Wales ready for a trip to Lowestoft, August 1921.

Along the North Parade large residential properties and hotels were being built on the western side, facing the sea. Strict control prevented any extension of entertainment along this part of the sea front but tennis courts and bowling greens were allowed on the seaward side. In 1926 the Ornamental Gardens and Boating Lake opened and two years later the Waterways were completed, both schemes carried out to improve the facilities the town could offer its visitors and at the same time provide work for the unemployed under the Government National Relief Fund.

The town was now advertising itself as a Conference Centre having been host in the 1930's to the National Union of Teachers, the Conservative and Unionist Association and the National Liberal Federation. In 1934 the Johnnie Walker whisky company erected a large cricket score board in the Wellington Pier gardens for the summer season as England played Australia for the Ashes. This was a huge success, the gardens being packed (mostly with men) as the scoreboard, which was connected to the cricket ground by telephone, displayed the latest score and other finer details of the game. In addition to the river, broads and sea trips the *Queen of the Channel* offered day trips to Ostend (see page 62). The ship sailed from South Quay in 1937 and the Fishwharf in 1938 and 1939. This service finished with the outbreak of war and the ship was subsequently sunk in the Dunkirk evacuation in 1940.

In the 1939 guide the Wellington Pier show 'Come to the Show' advertised seat prices at 2/6, 2/-, 1/6, and 1/- (12$\frac{1}{2}$p, 10p, 7$\frac{1}{2}$p and 5p) while the Victoria Hotel, now the Carlton, offered inclusive terms from 15/- to 19/6 per day (75p to 97$\frac{1}{2}$p). A typical small guest house in Wellesley Road offered board residence from 35/- (£1.75) per week or bed and breakfast from 4/6 (24p) per day.

The 1939 season was however to have an abrupt end with the outbreak of war in September. Seaside holidays came to an end for the next six years as the town became heavily fortified as a 'front line town'. The Marine Parade was out of bounds, the beaches mined and all places of entertainment were closed on government orders. Many venues such as the Hippodrome were requisitioned by the military and all thoughts of holidays were put on hold.

The Scenic Railway and Joy Wheel were the main attractions on the site which was later to become the Pleasure Beach, seen here c1912.

The Giant Slide and Scenic Railway in the 1930's. Private car ownership was beginning to become popular and the beginnings of 'parking problems' at peak times. Also at the Pleasure Beach at this time was a Miniature Railway, just visible on the left.

The open air Bathing Pool which opened in 1922 and closed in 1979.

GREAT YARMOUTH'S
GREAT SEA WATER
BATHING POOL

Manager to the Corporation   -   E. H. GOWER.

300 feet Long by 75 feet Wide. Depth from 3 feet to 8 feet.
Standard Diving Boards from 1 to 5 Metres.

LIGHT REFRESHMENTS

CHARGES :

To Bathe, Adults   6d. with Costume & Towel **9d.**
  ,,   **Children 3d.** ,,   ,,   **6d.**
         Spectators   2d.

CHIEF GALA ATTRACTIONS for 1939
(Under A.S.A. Laws).

Thursday, July 13th—Grammar School
    ,,   ,,   20th—Elementary Schools
    ,,   .,   27th—Gt. Yarmouth Police
    ,,   Aug. 3rd—County Championships
Friday,   ,,   11th—Hospital Gala—including the
                  Men's Mile Championship of England
Saturday, ,,   19th—"Ulph" Cup Gala
Thursday, ,,   24th—Gt. Yarmouth S.C. Annual

This programme of Gala Attractions at the Bathing Pool would have just been completed when the summer attractions of 1939 were abruptly brought to an end by the outbreak of war in early September.

The Post War Years

When the Second World War was finally over the military authorities began the task of clearing mines from the beaches, removing the barricades erected along the Marine Parade and handing back the buildings they had requisitioned for the duration of the war. The town now looked forward to rebuilding its reputation as a leading holiday resort and the first post war official guide was issued in 1946. Limited to sixteen pages by the paper restrictions the guide did its best to encourage people back to the town and the Mayor at that time, Councillor J Beckett, wrote in the introduction:

> *"During the war years we were one of the country's front line towns, and for the greater part of that time Great Yarmouth was a Defence Area in which visitors were banned. We in Great Yarmouth and Gorleston are already preparing for the holiday needs of visitors from all parts of the country and we can offer you nearly all the attractions and entertainment which made the town so popular as a holiday resort before the war."*

Visitors found that the war had left many scars in the town, the Parish Church was in ruins and much of the town centre and old Row area had been destroyed; the Observation Tower, a landmark and popular pre war attraction on the sea front, had been removed for the war effort in 1941. The Pleasure Beach reopened in 1946 and among the shows to open that year was the Wellington Pier where a concert party type show was staged 'retaining all the jollity and friendliness of the old Pierrot shows'. In the Winter Gardens there was dancing to Maurice Iliffe and his Broadcasting Orchestra while the Municipal Orchestra played at the Marina. The Windmill Theatre (previously the Gem) opened in June 1946 and the Britannia Pier reopened with the New Britannia Revels. By August the gap that had been blown in the pier as a war time defence had been bridged and the Ocean Ballroom was able to reopen.

The 1948 Holidays With Pay Act gave many thousands of manual workers a fortnight's paid holiday each year and many could now afford one or two weeks at the seaside.

A 1949 Punch & Judy show on Yarmouth beach, a favourite with children of all ages but now considered politically incorrect. The Britannia Pier Ocean Ballroom and Pavilion were both to burn down five years later

The *Golden Galleon*, the *Queen of the Broads* and the *Resolute* all preparing to leave Stonecutters Quay for broads trips in the 1960's. The Steward & Patteson offices in the background were demolished in 1970 and Havenbridge House built on the site in 1973. The *Resolute* finished broads trips in 1967 and the *Queen of the Broads* in 1976.

The Playbill for the Regal Theatre, June 1949. Stars of BBC radio were the 'big names' at the seaside in the days before television personalities took over the summer shows The Regal was later to be renamed the ABC and then the Cannon before being demolished in 1989.

One of the newest attractions on the Marine Parade was the Marina open air theatre which had opened in July 1937. The southern end of this development consisted of a circular arena with seating for 3000 and a stage at the eastern side, the seating around the edge being under cover. The northern end of the complex comprised two Cumberland Turf Bowling Greens divided by a paved terrace with an ornamental cascading fountain. On the eastern side of this was a covered seating area. Today the bowling greens are the site of the Pirates Cove golf course. At the Marina Neville Bishop was to be the resident entertainer through to the 1960's, each year hosting the popular Battle of Britain Bathing Beauty Contest where the final winner was crowned by one of the leading stars appearing in the town that year. Each morning Uncle Neville's Children's Parties were a popular favourite. For a few years in the 1970's the Marina was used for a Wild West Show but eventually it was demolished and the present Marina Leisure Centre was built on the site, opening in 1981.

In 1948 board residence was being advertised at various Guest Houses from 11/6 to 15/6 per day while the Holkham Hotel was charging 10/6 for Bed & Breakfast. At the larger hotels the weekly rate was from 5 guineas with the Imperial Hotel charging $5\frac{1}{2}$ guineas (£5.75). From the industrial towns of the Midlands many people came in Wakes Weeks, each town having a different week during the summer months when all its factories closed down and almost the entire population headed for the seaside. Private car ownership was increasing throughout the 50's but the majority of holidaymakers travelled by train or coach. In the absence of a coach station Church Plain became the centre of such activity on summer Saturdays. The closure of Beach railway station in 1959 and the subsequent new coach station on the site relieved some of this town centre congestion.

In 1951 a new amusement park, Joyland, opened at the northern end of the Marine Parade and the following year the Ark was added, a seafront landmark which was replaced by a spaceship in 1983. The 'snails', always a popular ride, remain today. In 1955 live shows could be seen at the Royal Aquarium, Wellington Pier, Britannia Pier, Regal and Windmill while films could be seen at the Empire and Regent. Together with circus at the Hippodrome, repertory at the Little Theatre and bands at the Marina these gave visitors a wide choice of entertainment. Admission prices ranged from 3/- to 6/- (15p to 30p) per seat.

Baron's Paradium amusement arcade and the Goode's Hotel in 1953.

The trumpet player Eddie Calvert was the star of the Windmill summer show
for the 1956 season.

The 1950 Carnival procession float for the Windmill Theatre advertising the comedians Dan and Jim Sherry as stars of the Yarmouth Follies summer show.

League of Friends of the
Great Yarmouth & Gorleston Hospitals
(Registered under the Charities Act, 1960)

ANNUAL
GARDEN
FETE

Lucky № 3845

****

**THURSDAY,
31st JULY, 1969**

Northgate Hospital
Great Yarmouth

****

GRAND OPENING by
ENGELBERT HUMPERDINCK
Currently Starring at the A.B.C. Theatre, Great Yarmouth

at 2.30 p.m.

ADMISSION BY PROGRAMME **1/-**

For many years the annual Hospital Fete, held in the grounds of Northgate Hospital, was always opened by one of the stars from a summer show. In 1969 it was the turn of Engelbert Humperdinck who was appearing at the ABC for the season, several years before he was to become an International star.

From the 1950's caravans formed an alternative and new form of holiday accommodation. Lit by Calor gas and with no water, electricity or drainage connected to these small caravans they provided a basic do-it-yourself holiday. Above is the South Denes caravan site and below similar caravans were to be found on the North Denes at the Seashore Camp. Both pictures are in the mid 1960's.

Although the habit of sunbathing had begun in the 1930's it was still only the young, more liberated generation, who wore bathing costumes on the beach, the older generation continued to wear their Sunday best suits, shoes, socks and hats. To remove these items, however hot and uncomfortable it became, was strictly taboo for many in the 1950's.

The 1950's and the 1960's were to be the heyday of British seaside resorts but the advent of cheap foreign package holiday in the late 60's heralded a change as fewer people holidayed at home. Seaside resorts, with the unpredictable British weather, were now unpopular and in the 70's the slowdown of manufacturing industries in the Midlands led to the Wakes Weeks being phased out, adding to the problems of seaside resorts.

Seaside entertainment had continued to flourish, live shows with 'star names' from television reaching a peak in 1967 when the town offered a choice of Morecambe and Wise, Rolf Harris, Mike and Bernie Winters, Val Doonican, Arthur Askey, Mike Yarwood, Ruby Murray, Joe Henderson and Freddie and The Dreamers all in one season. A familiar character on the beach from 1927 until 1960 was the local sand artist Fred Bultitude, whose skills were captured in his sand sculptures of horses, famous people and events.

Caravans now provided an alternative form of holiday accommodation with large sites being developed on the Denes at either end of the town. Many hotels and public houses along the seafront were being converted to amusement arcades and in 1965 the Coastguard Station was demolished and the Tower complex built on the site. When first opened this had an ice rink on the ground floor, now replaced with shops. In 1967 the second of the town's railway stations, Southtown, closed and the next decade was to see a sharp decline in seaside holidays as increased car ownership gave people more mobility and freedom, a trend which has continued to this day. One of the largest developments on the Marine Parade in the 1990's was the Sea Life Centre, which opened in 1991. The following year the Sandpiper public house was converted to Treasureworld and the Temple of Doom but by 1999 this had become Harry Ramsden's Fish Restaurant. The traditional seaside 'bucket and spade' holiday is still popular and the facilities and amenities constantly change to keep pace with requirements, there is still a great demand 'to be beside the seaside'.

The Tower complex was built on the site of the Coastguard Station and opened in 1965. The adjacent Royal Standard is now the Mint Amusement Arcade.

The Bath Hotel in 1987 when the public bar was known as the Circus Tavern. Shortly after this the ground floor became the Flamingo Amusement Arcade and the name Bath Hotel disappeared. Unfortunately today there is no indication that this building and its predecessor in the mid eighteenth century formed the foundation of Yarmouth as a seaside resort.

Acknowledgements

This book is dedicated to the millions of holidaymakers who have over the years made Great Yarmouth and Gorleston the choice for their seaside holiday and to the earlier visitors who came to 'take the waters' and seek a remedy for a wide range of health problems.

The information included in this book has been taken from many sources but the original notes and researches of a local historian, the late Ted Goate, have been of particular importance. Many of the photographs also come from Ted's extensive collection. As with previous books my wife Jan has provided invaluable help in choosing the images that have been used and has provided the continuous encouragement that is required to produce a book of this nature.